MW00412402

How to Think Well, and Why:
The Awareness to Action Guide
to Clear Thinking
By Mario Sikora

OUR PROGRAMS

Awareness to Action International offers a variety
of leadership-development programs based on the
content presented here. Find out more about our
programs in the back of this book.
www.awarenesstoaction.com

**For More on Leadership or the Enneagram,
visit
*www.mariosikora.com***

Dedication

The future depends on the ability of young people to learn to be good thinkers. This book is dedicated to my four sons, Adrian, Alec, Alexei, and Andrei, and they are the readers I had in mind while writing it.

"How to Think Well, and Why: The Awareness to Action Guide to Clear Thinking"
By Mario Sikora

TABLE OF CONTENTS

THE NEED:

It is not in our nature to think clearly. A complex world demands that we do.

There is an entertaining experiment that trainers do when trying to make a point about self-perception: simply ask people in the group to raise their hand if they think they are an above-average driver. Invariably, a significant majority of hands will go up.

This happens in group after group. You can ask yourself the same question as you read this, and chances are you are mentally raising your hand as well.

Obviously, a significant majority of people cannot be *above-average* drivers—in any given activity, *half of us need to be below average*. Therefore, at least some of us are fooling ourselves.

I get a similar response when I ask people if they believe they think more clearly than the average person—almost everyone thinks they are logical, rational, and good at telling truth from falsehood. Most of us believe we think more clearly than the average person, but again, at least some of us must be wrong.

Further, even being a better-than-average thinker does not mean we are particularly good at thinking clearly because, in general, humans are not very good at this important activity. We don't always use logic, we allow our emotions to override our reason, we seek easy and simplistic answers for complicated questions.

We don't do these things because we are bad people, or even because we are particularly lazy—we do it because we are limited to using the brains that we have inherited from our ancestors, but we live with very different circumstances than they did.

Our distant ancestors lived in dangerous-but-relatively simple times. Their daily agenda was uncomplicated: find food, don't get eaten by a predator or killed by a rival, make babies. Our brains evolved in response to this environment, an environment where action and decisiveness were useful, but subtlety and complete accuracy were not critical. (More about this later.)

We do, of course, have the capacity to be logical and rational and to increase the accuracy of our conclusions, but it does not come as naturally to us as we might think. Thus, we need to learn, practice, and use tools for clear-thinking that may feel unnatural to us.

And those tools have never been more important: We live in a world where we are bombarded by false or misleading information that comes to us unbidden via the apps on our cell phones, where hucksters try to sell us unnecessary or even dangerous products on our televisions, and where politicians try to confuse us into complacency. We must be armed to defend ourselves from this onslaught.

In addition to protecting ourselves from others, we must learn to protect ourselves from our own biases, ignorance, and incorrect assumptions if we want to be good citizens, protect ourselves or our families, or run prosperous businesses.

This short guide is a first step in learning how to do just that.

THE NEED FOR LEADERS:

Success in the market relies on effective decision-making; effective decision-making relies on clear thinking.

I work with leaders as an executive coach and leadership-development consultant. The most-effective leaders I work with all understand the importance of good clear-thinking skills, and they all complain that those skills need to be taught more broadly.

The best leaders know that they have a particular responsibility to develop the skills of clear thinking and they work diligently at doing so. They know that every leader has the responsibility for the well-being of the people they lead. The leader of a company has a responsibility to protect the company, its employees, and its customers. The leader of a team has a responsibility for the people who report to him or her, and to the families of those people who depend on the company for their financial security.

Every decision, every choice, every judgment leaders make is influenced by their ability to think well and see the world *as it is* rather than how they want it to be or wish it were.

If you want to be a leader, you need to develop clear-thinking skills. Failing to do so, or neglecting the daily effort to be diligent in telling fact from fiction, is an abdication of leadership responsibility.

THE SOLUTION:

A structured approach to developing tools for clear thinking.

We can develop the skills for clear thinking using the five abilities of Awareness to Action (ATA) Clear-Thinking Framework.

Those five abilities are:

- The ability to establish antidotes and guardrails to help protect us from our non-conscious biases.
- The ability to rewrite our internal narratives in a way that both uses and helps overcome our habitual personality patterns.
- The ability to recognize and address cultural factors that can limit our perspective.
- The ability to create a plan for broad learning that reduces our ignorance.
- The ability to intellectually cut through the sea of misinformation we encounter each day.

This guidebook is an introduction to both the obstacles to clear thinking (discussed in Section 1) and the skills and tools needed to develop these five abilities (discussed in Section 2).

FIRST THINGS FIRST: *FOUNDATIONAL IDEAS*

We Need a Network of Models and Tools

We are bombarded with information every day, much of it low-quality or outright wrong. To be effective thinkers we need tools for sorting through information, identifying that which is flawed, and acting upon that which is valid.

The aim of this guidebook is to help people do this through providing a set of tools and concepts structured into five broad domains (antidotes and guardrails, personality, culture, education, and debunking).

These domains provide a framework to allow the individual to develop a flexible--but disciplined, structured, and interconnected--web of models, concepts, and tools that help us see clearly.

Subjective Experience, Objective Reality, and Epistemic Clarity

I know—big words. But good thinkers are not afraid of a few big words, especially if they are important words, so bear with me for a moment.

Oxford Dictionary identified "post-truth" as the word of the year in 2016, and defined it as "relating to or denoting circumstances in which objective facts are less influential in shaping public opinion than appeals to emotion and personal belief."

Many people consider reason, emotion, and intuition to be simply different "ways of knowing," and to some extent they are correct—we can learn much about the world from our emotions and intuition.

However, we run into trouble when we assume all "ways of knowing" are equal and interchangeable and we apply them to the wrong topics. We *feel* when we should *think* (and sometimes vice versa), we confuse beliefs and opinions for facts, we reject facts that make us feel bad.

There is a branch of philosophy called "epistemology" that is devoted to "ways of knowing," or how we can truly know those things we know. It recognizes that we humans each interpret the world through the filters of our subjectivity, but that we must develop tools for telling the difference between subjective experience and objective reality.

The heart of clear thinking lies in "epistemic clarity," the ability to tell the difference between subjective experience and objective reality, and to act accordingly.

It helps to remember:

- *Subjective Experience*: is what we call our unique, non-rational, and feeling-based responses to the world. For example, preferences in music, cuisine, politics, and aesthetics are all subjective.
- *Objective Reality*: is that which is true no matter how you *feel* about it. For example, our preferences regarding gravity, velocity, the spinning of the earth, and mathematical formulas are irrelevant; they are simple matters of fact whether we like them or not.
- *Epistemic Clarity*: is the ability to tell the difference between Subjective Experience and Objective Reality.

Keep This in Mind: The Brain Loves Stories

When trying to understand the workings of the mind, we have to always remember one fundamental fact: The brain loves to create stories.

Your brain is always filtering through data and turning it into a narrative. Doing so makes stress and uncertainty go away by fitting the data into some kind of understandable context, even if that context is completely fabricated.

This is not necessarily a bad thing—it is this ability that allows us to see repeated patterns and prepare for the future.

Unfortunately, our brains often have a difficult time distinguishing true stories from fake stories so we are often making up, without realizing it, explanations for things that happen to and around us that are simple and satisfying, but often wrong.

This creation and embrace of narratives reinforces many of the mind's other tricks that we will explore in the pages that follow.

SECTION 1:

THE OBSTACLES TO CLEAR THINKING

THE FIVE OBSTACLES

OBSTACLES TO CLEAR THINKING

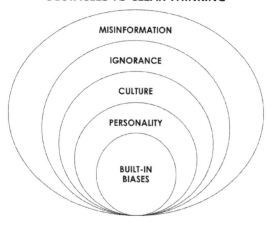

There are many factors that lead to our inability to see clearly. The Awareness to Action Clear-Thinking Framework identifies five factors that contribute to this inability. It starts with the fundamental structures of our brain, and then proceeds outward to "misinformation" (see figure above). While they can be addressed individually, it helps to know that they feed or reinforce each other from the inside out (i.e., personality is reinforced by our built-in biases), but each also reinforces those preceding it (i.e., misinformation reinforces ignorance, the detrimental elements of culture, etc.).

The solutions for overcoming these obstacles are found in Section 2.

BUILT-IN BIASES: THE ROOT OF OUR TROUBLES

We like to think we see the world clearly, that our perceptions are reliable, that our thinking is logical.

When we take a moment to step back and look at ourselves, however, we realize that this is not always the case. In fact, we often see the world through a variety of filters, our perceptions can be unreliable, and our thinking can be logically flawed.

This is not a new observation, of course; many ancient wisdom traditions are rooted in the idea that we are hindered by illusions and must learn to see clearly in order to become "enlightened." The modern scientific literature on the inaccuracy and dysfunction of the brain is also vast.

In order to understand how our brains fools us, it helps to understand one fundamental fact about the evolution of the brain: **the brain evolved to help us survive, not to help us accurately comprehend the world around us**.

Evolution follows a very simple algorithm: *That which increases the chances of reproduction tends to get reproduced.* This very simple, but very elegant, algorithm, constantly repeated over unimaginably vast amounts of time, accounts for all the characteristics of all the species on our planet.

Our brain has evolved over eons and natural selection has "equipped" it with characteristics to help us survive and reproduce. Sometimes, those very same characteristics actually inhibit our ability to see the world around us accurately. Natural selection has saddled us with intuitions that keep us safe or make our lives easier, and it has wired us so that we will be certain of the accuracy of these intuitions, *even when* the intuitions are not accurate.

We humans are pattern-spotting marvels, and we are constantly spotting patterns whether they exist or not. When we intuit a pattern, our brain disinclines us to doubt ourselves because it is generally more advantageous to stubbornly believe we see a pattern where it doesn't exist than it is to doubt that the pattern is real.

To illustrate, let's go back in time. Four of our distant relatives, let's call them Fred, Barney, Wilma, and Betty, are walking along and hear a rustle in the bushes. They turn to look in the direction of the noise and Fred and Wilma perceive the pattern of a lion in the bushes, and they run away. Barney thinks he sees something too, but says to himself, "It could be a lion, but I'm not sure." He trots a small distance but stops to wait and see if he was right in his assumption. Betty doesn't even see the pattern and wonders why everyone is running.

It turns out that the rustling in the bushes was just the wind, and Betty later has a good laugh at the expense of Fred and Wilma when telling the story to others.

The next day, the four are out for another walk. Again, there is a rustle. Fred and Wilma see the pattern of a lion, and despite Betty's mocking of them the previous day, again they run. Barney takes a few steps but stops, again, not implicitly trusting his intuitions. True to form, Betty doesn't see the pattern and stays in place.

This time, however, the rustling is not the wind; it is a lion. Fred and Wilma get away and survive to have babies, most of whom share their brains' traits. Betty, on the other hand, becomes the lion's lunch. Barney survives this time but, lacking an implicit faith in his pattern-recognizing intuition, is not long for this world and leaves few or no offspring.

We have these accuracy-inhibiting characteristics "engineered" into our brain because false positives, such as those that Fred and Wilma had a tendency toward, cost us very little. However, false negatives, such as that to which Betty was prone, can be fatal.

Doubting our intuitions, such as Barney did, can do more harm than good. The simple algorithm determines that those with a bias toward seeing patterns that did not actually exist and were overly certain about their intuitions had a better chance of reproducing. We are their offspring. We share their traits–we sometimes see things that aren't there and we are overly sure of our naive intuitions.

I don't want to paint too bleak a picture of the situation. In general, the brain does a pretty good job at assessing and interpreting our environment. We are right most of the time. But we are wrong enough that we need help, and this is why the tools related to good, rigorous thinking are critical. They help us get from being "pretty good" in our assessments to "very good."

Two Systems of the Brain

Daniel Kahneman's book "Thinking Fast and Slow" has helped popularize the idea that we have two general cognitive systems for processing information. Kahneman's book is one of many popular volumes published in recent years that describe what we have learned from the cognitive sciences over the past few decades about the workings of the mind. These insights can provide very useful insights in how to use the Enneagram to create change.

System 1, as Kahneman describes, is fast, heuristic-based thinking. It relies on deeply rooted, non-conscious mental models that allow us to make quick decisions without having to think any more than absolutely necessary, if we think at all. The beauty of System 1 is that it is generally good enough to help us meet the basic demands of daily life without requiring us to expend too much energy.

Unfortunately, System 1 is not always accurate. While it is often very effective for solving short-term problems, it can cause us to act in ways that undermine us in the long run.

System 2 is slow, rational thinking. It is the conscious, deliberate weighing of variables and data and considering of long-term consequences. It is more accurate, but it also requires more caloric energy and thus takes a physical toll on us, so we tend to minimize its use. (Ever notice how tired you are after a long period of concentrated thinking or attention? This is the result of System 2 causing the brain to burn a lot of energy.)

Broadly, the existence of these two systems means that we have access to two thinking modes that both serve a useful end, but we sometimes use one when we should use the other–with unfortunate results. For example, we may come to regret relying on System 2 slow thinking when we accidentally step out into traffic or relying on System 1 fast thinking when deciding to buy a used car.

Understanding Cognitive Dissonance

Cognitive dissonance is the psychological stress caused by contradictory ideas battling for space in our minds. Such tension causes us stress and anxiety, so our mind seeks to dispel it as quickly as possible. It does so by finding a way to reject one of the ideas without due consideration—usually the one that contradicts our currently held beliefs.

The root of cognitive dissonance is in our attempt to maintain our self-esteem. We all want to think well of ourselves. Few of us see ourselves as bad people, even if we sometimes make mistakes. When we do something that contradicts our perception of ourselves, we experience the discomfort of cognitive dissonance. We then fall victim to a variety of cognitive biases— automatic mental models that can distort our thinking. Embracing these biases is the brain's way of dispelling the dissonance and protecting our positive view of ourselves.

For example, if we think we are doing well in our job and we get negative feedback in a 360 assessment, it is tempting to rationalize the feedback by attributing ignorance or malice to the source of the comments we don't like, or to assume that the comments are based on insufficient or flawed data. If we design a product we truly believe in but it is not well-received by the market, it is tempting to blame the users or believe that our product is "too ahead of its time" rather than think there might be something wrong with the product.

It is helpful to understand that cognitive dissonance and our attempts to mitigate it happen below the level of our awareness—we don't do it on purpose. Our brain identifies the tension before we consciously register it and it sets us on the course of some process to make it go away by applying a cognitive bias. We all do it, and we don't realize it. We don't do it because we are bad people, it happens unless we train ourselves to look for signs of cognitive dissonance (such as, the stress we feel when confronted with an idea we don't like) and take steps to avoid falling into the traps of our mitigating biases.

See Section 2 for tips on addressing cognitive dissonance.

Confirmation Bias

"Confirmation bias" is the tendency we all have to see what we *want* to see or what we *expect* to see.

It is the tendency to embrace evidence that fits our point of view (referred to as *biased assimilation*) and to ignore or minimize evidence that does not fit (referred to as *cognitive discounting*).

While there are many cognitive biases, confirmation bias is the one that can be the most common and problematic.

Confirmation bias is what causes us to be overly optimistic about projects, products, or people.

At the same time, confirmation bias can make us ignore signals that we should pay more attention to something we are dismissing.

Confirmation bias is a constant threat to clear and effective thinking. The best thinkers safeguard themselves by asking some simple questions:

- How do I know this to be true?
- What evidence is there that I could be wrong?

They also take pride in changing their mind based on new evidence.

A List of Common Cognitive Biases

- *Affect heuristic*: a mental shortcut in which current emotion—fear, pleasure, surprise, etc.—influences decisions.
- *Anchoring or focalism*: the tendency to rely too heavily on the first piece of information offered (the "anchor") when making decisions.
- *Automation bias*: the propensity for humans to over-rely on suggestions from automated decision-making systems.
- *Availability heuristic*: the tendency to rely on immediate examples that come to mind when evaluating a situation or decision. Overvalues things that can be recalled easily, even if they are less accurate or useful pieces of data than things that are less easy to recall.
- *Bandwagon effect*: the tendency to embrace ideas, beliefs, fads or trends that are popular with others.
- *Clustering illusion*: the tendency to see random clustering in a small sample as a pattern reflecting a larger trend.
- *Confirmation bias*: is the tendency to non-consciously embrace or interpret information in a way that confirms one's preexisting beliefs or hypotheses.

- *Curse of knowledge*: the tendency of experts to overestimate an audience's or another person's depth of knowledge of a given topic.
- *Escalation of commitment*: when an individual or group—faced with increasingly negative outcomes from some decision, action, or investment—continues the same behavior rather than change course.
- *Framing effect*: the tendency of the presentation method of the information to shape the perception of the information.
- *Gambler's fallacy*: the belief that if something happens more frequently than normal during a given period it will happen less frequently in the future, or vice versa.
- *Halo effect*: when an observer's overall impression of a person, company, brand, or product influences the observer's feelings and thoughts about that entity's character or specific properties. The tendency to assume higher competence among more-attractive people is a good example.
- *Hindsight bias*: the tendency, after an event has occurred, to unjustifiably see the event as having been predictable.
- *Illusion of control*: the tendency for people to overestimate their ability to control events.
- *Loss aversion*: the tendency to significantly prefer avoiding losses to acquiring equivalent gains.
- *Negativity bias*: the tendency of negative experiences to have a substantially greater impact on people's perceptions than neutral or positive experiences.
- *Normalcy bias*: the tendency to underestimate the possibility of disasters and minimize their potential impact, assuming that things will function basically like they always have. Leads to a lack of planning for emergencies.

- *Optimism bias*: the belief that the individual is at less risk of experiencing negative events than others are.
- *Ostrich effect*: the tendency to avoid bad news; especially when related to finances.
- *Outcome bias*: an error made when evaluating the quality of a decision when the outcome of that decision is already known.
- *Overconfidence effect*: when a person's subjective confidence in his or her judgments is reliably greater than the objective accuracy of those judgements, especially when confidence is relatively high. Similar to Dunning-Kruger effect in which people who are less competent tend to over-rate their competence and people who are more competent tend to underrate their competence.
- *Planning fallacy*: the tendency to underestimate the time and effort needed to complete a future task.
- *Regression fallacy*: the assumption that circumstances returned to normal (regression to the mean) due to corrective actions taken rather than natural fluctuations.
- *Selective memory*: the brain's tendency to select, delete, or distort memories without our awareness.
- *Status quo bias*: a preference for the current state of affairs, and tendency to use the status quo as the baseline reference point despite longer term trends that demonstrate otherwise.
- *Sunk cost fallacy*: an unwillingness or resistance to cut one's losses, even in the face of evidence that further investment will lead to greater loss.
- *Temporal discounting*: the tendency of people to discount rewards when they are farther in the future or the past.

RELATED PHENOMENA

In addition to these cognitive biases, there are a number of psychological tendencies that can impair our thinking. Some are listed here.

The Dunning-Kruger Effect

The Dunning-Kruger Effect (DKE) is the phenomenon where the people who are least competent in a given area are the least able to judge their competence and the most likely to be overconfident in their expertise. They will also be least likely to be able to recognize competence in others, so they tend to ignore or dismiss experts because they don't actually recognize their expertise.

Conversely, those with high expertise will be likely to underestimate their competence, primarily because they know how complicated their domain is and they know that they have a lot more to learn. True expertise often leads to humility.

Humans are wired for certainty. Our brains don't like loose ends or open questions, so it seeks to wrap things up in neat little stories that make our existential anxieties go away.

At the same time, our brain is wired for energy efficiency, meaning that it will seek the simplest way to make uncertainty go away. It creates stories about the world, giving us a sense of closure and certainty but blocking out new or conflicting information. It will stop us from seeking information that would cause us to spend time and energy reconciling our beliefs with the facts.

The less information we have about a topic, the more simplistic our story about that topic is and the less willing we are to put in the time and energy to becoming informed and competent. The more ignorant we are, the more our brain will fight against seeing our ignorance because, by the logic of the brain's intuitive cost-benefit analysis, it makes more sense to fool us with overconfidence than to invest the energy into learning all the things we need to learn to build competence.

Motivated Reasoning

Motivated reasoning is a phenomenon that incorporates a number of cognitive biases such as *biased assimilation* and *identity-protective cognition.* It helps people reason their way toward a(n often non-consciously) predetermined conclusion. It is a modern and fancy way of restating Hume's assertion that our feelings form our conclusions and our intellect finds a way to support them.

Motivated reasoning is frequently on display whenever people are discussing issues to which they are either ideologically identified or in which they have a personal stake in the outcome. It is the true believers of every stripe who will take any piece of data and twist it to support their point of view and deny any contradicting evidence, no matter how strong that evidence is.

It is important to realize that we are *all* afflicted with a tendency toward motivated reasoning. We *all* have self-interests, prejudices, and emotionally held beliefs that we easily reason our way toward, and while we can sometimes easily see it in others it is very difficult to see motivated reasoning in ourselves. This last thought should stop us in our smugness when criticizing others' thinking and keep us humble about our own.

Further, motivated reasoning is not just seen in social, political, or faith matters. It affects almost every decision we make and it can influence the way decisions are made in organizations. People have a strong tendency to unconsciously argue toward a conclusion that befits their worldview.

Leaps of Inference

An unjustified leap of inference is drawing a conclusion that may not necessarily flow from the premises used to arrive at that conclusion. For example, just because I can safely jump off a curb and jump off a chair does not mean I can safely jump off a cliff. Assuming I could would be a leap too far.

Leaps of inference are much more common than we realize. They are often the root of conspiracy thinking or questionable assertions about history or science. They are a mechanism that allows us to embrace beliefs we want to believe but for which we don't have solid evidence.

Naïve Realism

We have the views we do about the world around us because those views make sense to us. Whether it is something we have thought a lot about or whether we are following our initial gut reaction, everyone believes they believe what any reasonable person would believe given the same set of facts.

Psychologists call this phenomenon "naïve realism," which Thomas Gilovich and Lee Ross describe as "the seductive and compelling sense that one sees the world the way it is, not as a subjective take on the world" in their excellent book, "The Wisest One in the Room."

Our brains manufacture certainty in a way that convinces us we interpret the world in a way that any "reasonable" person would, and we don't realize that much of what we believe is highly subjective ("the thing as we know it") and not necessarily a match to reality ("the thing as it is").

The importance of this simple idea cannot be overstated—we all think we are right about how we see the world and that anyone who thinks differently is either ill-informed or ill-intentioned. The greater the disparity between different points of view, and the more important a particular belief is to us, the more likely we are to attribute negative qualities to people who believe differently. The more you and I disagree on an important topic, the more likely you are to assume that I am not just stupid, but that I am a bad person as well. (And I will probably fall into the same trap...)

The Fundamental Attribution Error

The *fundamental attribution error* is the common tendency to view *our* less-admirable actions as a reasonable response to our circumstances but see *other people's* actions as a mark of their character structure. When we misbehave it is because we had a *bad day*; when others misbehave it is because they are a *bad person*.

Combine this with the closely related *correspondence bias*—our tendency to assume a broad quality of another's character based on one or a few actions or traits—and it is no wonder that humans tend to live in a world of simplistic stereotypes.

Self-Deception and the Enigma of Reason

As much as we like to think we are rational and evidence-based, most of our arguments are actually attempts to rationalize something that we intuitively feel is true and convince others of the merit of our intuitions.

Cognitive scientists Dan Sperber and Hugo Mercier have an explanation for this phenomenon that they call "the argumentative theory of reasoning," and we would do well to understand their ideas if we truly want to understand how our minds work.

At the root of this theory, which is gaining traction with other cognitive scientists, is the idea that the brain did not evolve as a tool for accurate understanding of our world; it evolved to equip us to survive more effectively. They believe that all the cognitive biases built into our minds are not glitches in the system, but features of the system that serve their purpose very effectively.

Survival requires getting the things we need and want from life, and we often do that more effectively when we can convince others to see the wisdom of our point of view (whether our point of view holds the actual truth or not...). Thus, our capacity to reason is not a tool for finding truth, or even for solving problems; our capacity to reason is a tool for convincing others of the rightness of our views so we can get what we want.

Further, Sperber and Mercier agree with cognitive scientists such as Robert Trivers, who makes the case in his book "The Folly of Fools," that humans have developed the ability to deceive others in order to effectively compete for resources. Further, the most effective way to convince others is to first fool ourselves into believing whatever story will justify our initial emotion-based intuitions. In short, we easily fool ourselves into believing convenient falsehoods that serve our selfish purposes, and then we reason skillfully for what we have fooled ourselves into believing. The more skilled we are at reasoning, the more we convince ourselves that those intuitions are correct.

People who reason skillfully are often able to convince others of their "rightness," frequently to the detriment of the one being convinced. Such people are what are commonly referred to as "influencers" and they often rise to leadership positions—with both positive and negative consequences.

28

The key implication of the argumentative theory of reasoning is that we can't always trust our own reasoning and we need objective, external tools to help us uncover the ways we may be deceiving ourselves. Sperber and Mercier also point out that the group needs objective methods to protect its members from charismatic, but wrong, leaders and influencers.

Simply adhering to what the boss says or following the most charismatic person in the room can be a recipe for disaster. The same thing that the great physicist Richard Feynman said about science applies to business as well: "it is important that you don't fool yourself, and you are the easiest person to fool."

PERSONALITY

The Enneagram: Patterns of Habitual Personality

"Personality" is a word with multiple meanings. For our purpose, our personality is the habitual pattern of thoughts, feelings, and behaviors that we rely on to address the typical challenges we face during the course of life. It can also serve as a filter that helps us streamline and simplify both our perception of the world and our response to it.

Understanding our personality style helps us see past that filter, and also understand the filters that impede others' ability to see clearly.

The Enneagram is the most powerful model available for understanding personality styles. The system identifies three instinctual biases, or deeply rooted patterns of attention and values, and nine strategies for satisfying those values. (Visit www.AbouttheEnneagram.com for more information on this system.)

A Warning About the Enneagram and "Typologies"

Because this is a guide to clear thinking, we would be remiss not to point out some of the dangers related to personality typologies. Most of them are not supported by science and there is a very real danger of using them to stereotype people, taking us even further away from clear thinking.

The Enneagram, in particular, is problematic because it is an "open-source" model with many different approaches. It is easy to find multiple interpretations of and claims about the Enneagram, and some of those fall victim to the biases and fallacies described in this guide.

However, used appropriately, the Enneagram is a powerful tool for helping us see our innate biases related to patterns of thinking, feeling, and behaving. The "Awareness to Action Approach" to the Enneagram is an approach to the system that has been field-tested in organizations of all sizes across the globe over the last 20 years. It has been updated and revised to be consistent with both practical experience and the latest science about human nature.

No model of personality, including the Enneagram, should be seen as a "truth;" they should be viewed as a guide to remind us to look at our patterns of bias and to correct for those biases. The Enneagram should not be used as a means to limit ourselves or others, but as a tool for helping to expand our self-awareness and our understanding of the people around us.

Here is a brief overview of the Awareness to Action Approach to the Enneagram. It has been developed by the author and is based on over two decades of working with leaders on five continents. You can find more information at www.AbouttheEnneagram.com.

The Awareness to Action Enneagram

People with all sorts of personalities can be successful at work and in life. There are successful introverts and successful extroverts, successful optimists and successful pessimists. Our personality style doesn't determine our success, but while it is often the source of many of our strengths, it can create blind spots and obstacles that can hold us back.

The value of personality models is that they give us a framework for leveraging strengths and more-quickly recognizing blind spots and obstacles. A good model can also provide us with roadmaps for overcoming those blind spots and obstacles.

No model of personality styles does those things better than the Enneagram.

Over the course of my 20 years as an executive coach and consultant I've encountered a lot of personality models; none of them come close to the Enneagram in terms of real-world applicability and usefulness. That is why it has become such a central part of my work—it helps get the results my clients expect.

The word "Enneagram" literally refers to a diagram with nine intersecting lines creating nine points enclosed in a circle ("ennea" is Greek for nine, "gram" for drawing). This diagram is used to represent nine personality styles and the interrelationships among those styles.

There are two dimensions of personality described by the Enneagram. The first is our inherent system of instinctual values—what we habitually focus our attention on and what is important to us. The second dimension is the strategies we use to satisfy those values. In other words, the Enneagram helps us understand what is important to people (the instinctual biases) and how they habitually go about getting those things that are important to them (the strategies).

(Note: Most approaches to the Enneagram focus more on the nine strategies—thus the "ennea"—and view the instinctual values as a secondary matter. At the Awareness to Action Institute we understand that both dimensions are important and focus equally on both of them.)

Before we explain each of these dimensions further, we should take a moment to understand a bit about the way the mind works.

The brain requires an amount of energy that is far out of proportion to its mass. That three pounds or so between your ears requires about 20% of your energy expenditure. In order to minimize the energy it spends, the brain has evolved ways to make its work easier.

One important way it does this is by habituating behavior—taking behaviors that work well and making them automatic—and by relying on patterns of behavior that can be repeated in as many situations as possible. This is why we have personality "styles"—they are one of the brain's techniques for applying the same pattern to multiple situations in an effort to save energy and increase efficiency.

Thus, when we talk about dimensions of personality styles we are talking about habitual patterns that, somewhere in the past, some part of our brains decided were effective.

There is nothing wrong with having habits—they can be very effective in helping us get through life without having to face every situation as if for the first time. But we can also find ourselves falling into behavioral patterns that worked in the past but might not be quite right for a particular situation we face today, sometimes even causing more harm than good. Working with the Enneagram helps us recognize when we are using outdated or ill-suited patterns and it helps us develop the flexibility to free ourselves from them.

Dimension 1: Three Instinctual Biases

Dimension 1 of the Enneagram personality model is the three instinctual biases. The instinctual biases are deeply ingrained tendencies to find certain aspects of life more important than others and to focus our attention accordingly. These instinctual concerns fall into three broad domains. We all pay some attention to each of these domains, but we tend to focus on them unequally and we are biased toward one of the domains noticeably more than the others.

Those domains are:

- *Preserving*: focused on "nesting and nurturing" and on ensuring that fundamental survival needs are met for things like food, water, clothing, shelter, and overall safety from harm.

- *Navigating*: focused on "orienting to the group" and on building alliances, creating trust and reciprocity, and understanding how oneself and others fit into the group.
- *Transmitting*: focused on "attracting and bonding" and on passing genes, beliefs, values, interests, and worldview to others in order to make them carriers of that information.

What we value influences what we focus on at work. These instinctual biases have a dramatic effect on how we interact with coworkers, how we lead, how teams function, and more. (See, for example, the list of leadership tendencies below). People of different instinctual biases will focus on different tasks and objectives and we are often surprised when people place their priorities somewhere other than where we do. Such value discrepancies often a significant source of miscommunication and conflict in the workplace. Understanding the influence of the instinctual biases can help us reduce them.

Common Leadership Traits of Each Instinctual Bias

Preserving leaders in general:

- Good at preserving the "nest": ensuring their own security and the security of co-workers and subordinates they are responsible for.
- Good at playing Devil's advocate and challenging ideas that may not be fully thought-through. However, can be risk-averse, resistant to change and new ways of doing things.
- Good at ensuring that administrative issues are in order and that procedures are being implemented and followed.
- Comfortable in organizations that need stability and order; they may struggle in a fast changing environment.
- May be too introverted: focus on tasks rather than interpersonal issues.
- May lack charisma; can seem detached rather than inspirational.

Navigating leaders in general:

- Naturally drawn to issues related to group dynamics and interpersonal communication.
- Track group cohesion and status changes.
- Attuned to organizational politics, intuitively knowing which levers to pull in order to move projects around obstacles.
- Ability to instinctively read the pulse of the group, build the consensus, and know who needs to be pushed, who need to be nurtured, and who the influencers are.
- Good at the "forming" stage of team dynamics, where the group is finding its identity and ways of working together.
- Good at big picture and strategic thinking.
- Can be too focused on the political dynamics of the group, spending more time on the politics than on the organization's ultimate business goal.
- May have poor administrative capabilities.
- Less comfortable in difficult individual interaction and personnel decisions (e.g. addressing underperformance, firing, reprimanding).

Transmitting leaders in general:

- Often charismatic and bold.
- Good at articulating a goal or vision and moving others toward it, seducing some and driving others as necessary.
- Intuitively understand the mind of the market and the customer; persuasive seller of the products, company or dream.
- Good at building relationships with customers, channel partners and strategic allies.
- Highly competitive (alpha male or female of the group).
- Good at the start-up phase of a business, when the workforce needs an inspiring vision to rally around.

- May place too much focus on themselves, their accomplishments and their desirable qualities. May neglect career development of subordinates.
- Self-focus may seem to put own interests before company/employees.

Dimension 2: The Nine Strategies

There are nine distinct adaptive strategies for satisfying our instinctual concerns (again, the "Ennea" in "Enneagram" means nine). The strategies are consistent patterns of feeling, thinking, and doing that influence our interactions with the world around us (and the people in it). As with the instinctual domains, we use each of the nine strategies to a greater or lesser degree, but we use one of them more than the others. Because of the habitual overuse, we call this the "preferred" strategy. Each point on the Enneagram drawing represents one of these strategies.

In Enneagram parlance, the different personality styles are referred to by the number at which their preferred strategy is placed. Thus, someone whose preferred strategy is "striving to feel perfect" is referred to as an Ennea-type One; someone "striving to feel connected" is an Ennea-type Two, etc. (See below for a very brief overview of the nine strategies. You can find much more at our website.)

When we combine the instinctual biases with the preferred strategies we get three distinct versions of each Ennea-type. For example, an Ennea-type Three has a preferred strategy of "striving to feel outstanding," but a "Preserving Three" will non-consciously emphasize feeling outstanding in the preserving domain while a "Navigating Three" will emphasize feeling outstanding in the navigating domain.

It might seem simple, but understanding both dimensions provides profound insights into our own fundamental motivations and tendencies and those of the people we work with.

The Nine Ennea-Type Strategies

Ennea-Type One: Striving to Feel Perfect. They are often models of decorum, clear logic and appropriate behavior. They focus on rules, procedures and making sure that they are always doing the "right thing." When they overdo their Striving to feel Perfect they can become critical, judgmental and unwilling to take risks. Under stress, Ones may fear that if they have too much fun they will become irresponsible.

Ennea-Type Two: Striving to Feel Connected. They are often selfless, caring and nurturing. They focus on helping others meet their needs; they build rapport easily and enjoy finding a common bond with others. When they overdo their Striving to feel Connected they may fail to take care of their own needs and end up becoming emotionally dependent on others. Under stress, Twos may fear that if they are not closely connected to others they will become isolated.

Ennea-type Three: Striving to Feel Outstanding. They work hard to exceed standards and to be successful in whatever they undertake. They place high value on productivity and presenting an image of being a winner in whatever environment they are in. When they overdo their Striving to feel Outstanding they may become attention seeking and may value image over substance. When stressed, Threes may fear that if they are not making great efforts to be excellent they will become mediocre.

Ennea-Type Four: Striving to Feel Unique. They generally approach their lives creatively, in fresh and interesting ways. They gravitate toward things and experiences that are elegant, refined, or unusual. When they overdo their Striving to feel Unique they may feel misunderstood, and they may withdraw from others and become isolated. When stressed, Fours may fear that if they do not put their own special touch on their world and their experiences their individuality will become repressed.

Ennea-type Five: Striving to Feel Detached. They are observant, logical and generally reserved. They focus on problem solving, innovative ideas, and data gathering. When they overdo their Striving to feel Detached they can end up being dull—out of touch with their experiences and emotions. When stressed, Fives may fear that if they do not remain detached and guarded they will become uncontrolled.

Ennea-Type Six: Striving to Feel Secure. They find security in being part of something bigger than themselves, such as a group or tradition. They are careful, responsible and protective of the welfare of the group. They focus on maintaining consistency, tradition and cohesion. When they overdo their Striving to feel Secure they may fail to take the risks necessary for high performance and settle for mediocrity. When stressed, Sixes may fear that if they relax their guard they will be vulnerable to possible dangers.

Ennea-Type Seven: Striving to Feel Excited. They are upbeat, enthusiastic, optimistic, and curious. They focus on possibilities and options and keeping others entertained. When they overdo their Striving to feel Excited they may fail to follow-through, become easily distracted, and act irresponsibly. When stressed, Sevens may fear that if they do not fill their heads with many thoughts they will miss out on something.

Ennea-Type Eight: Striving to Feel Powerful. They are action-oriented self-starters who love to be in charge. They focus on getting things done and overcoming obstacles that may lie in their way. When they overdo their Striving to feel Powerful they may not adhere to the rules or norms that others expect them to follow and their behavior can become uncontrolled. When stressed, Eights may fear that if they become too connected to others or experience their own emotions too deeply they will become dependent on others.

Ennea-Type Nine: Striving to Feel Peaceful. They are calm, pleasant, and charming. They focus on maintaining a sense of inner harmony by minimizing their own needs and concentrating on the needs of others. When they overdo their Striving to feel Peaceful they can become passive, relying on others to make decisions for them. When stressed, Nines may fear that if they place too much importance on themselves they will be seen as attention seeking.

CULTURE

The Pull of Culture

We are becoming ever-more globalized. While most of our ancestors often rarely encounter anyone outside the tribe or strayed far from their homes, we live in an age where we can board an airplane and be almost anywhere in the world the next day. It is an age of multinational organizations and multi-lingual people, and there is a good chance that most of your possessions were made somewhere far away. This means that understanding culture grows more important every day.

One way of understanding "culture" is to see it as a given group's implicitly or explicitly agreed-upon way of solving the problems of group living. Culture is the source of most human accomplishment; it is the source of our shared sense of meaning, accountability, and responsibilities; it is what allows us to survive together. The downside of culture is that it can provide another filter that makes it difficult to see objectively.

Cultures develop at the level of the family, the team, the organization, the region, and the country. Each of us is the product of multiple overlapping cultural factors that shape our behavior in ways that can be difficult to identify.

Culture can shape many aspects of how we interpret the world.

Culture can shape our relationship with time—people some cultures live in "clock time" ("The bus will be here at 10:20 am"), others live in "event time" ("Don't worry, the bus will get here when it gets here").

While cultural differences are countless and varied, some common dimensions for understanding culture include:

- *Collectivist* ("The well-being of the group is what matters most") vs *individualist* ("The well-being of the individual is what matters most"),
- *Assertive* ("Here is what I can do") vs *humble* ("I did not do much"),
- *Low Uncertainty Avoidance* ("Whatever happens will happen; new things are opportunities") vs *High Uncertainty Avoidance* ("We have to make efforts ensure that bad things don't happen; new things are threats."),
- *Short-term view* ("We need to worry about what is happening now") vs *long-term view* ("We have to worry about what will happen in the future"), and
- *Small-power distance* ("The powerful are responsible to the masses") and *large-power distance* ("The masses must obey the powerful").

Each culture exists somewhere on a continuum in each of these areas, and each culture has its own unique profile. People from cultures with similar characteristics find it easier to connect with each other; the more different our cultures are, the more foreign we will feel to each other.

IGNORANCE

We Don't Know What We Don't Know

No one knows everything. Ignorance—the lack of knowledge—often impedes our ability to think effectively. When we lack general knowledge the facts we *do* know are not understood in their full context; their significance is diminished. A diverse and interesting world, and the solutions to many of our problems, are often right in front of us, but hidden by a veil of ignorance.

Ironically, we live in a time where all the facts in the world are available to us via the internet. We carry the greatest library ever assembled right on our cellphones. But it comes with a drawback.

Socrates argued 2500 years ago that the written word was intellectually harmful to us—the fact that we could write something down meant that we didn't have to remember it. Thus, when we needed to know something, the knowledge wasn't available to us unless we knew where it was written down. It created a state of ignorance in which we may not know what we don't know and therefore not know how to find the insights we need.

One can argue that the net benefit of writing and reading is positive (I certainly would), but Socrates had a point—without a broad base of general knowledge to carry with us in our minds we are destined to remain ignorant, even if the answers we seek lie in the devices in our pockets. We simply don't know what questions to ask.

Broad general knowledge, however, provides a lattice-work in which the world contains a richness and depth unavailable to the ignorant. The knowledgeable see connections and gain insights others can't even imagine, and they know the questions to ask and places to look to find the answers others will never see.

MISINFORMATION

Fake News, Social Media, and the "Post-Truth" World

Fake news and distorted truths are nothing new: humans have always been prone to share and believe rumors, tall-tales, and fantastical stories.

Never before, however, have such fictions been so amplified and accelerated as they are today due to technology and human interconnectedness. And never before have the consequences been so dire.

Misinformation threatens our health, our safety, our financial security, and the future of the planet and our peaceful existence on it.

I don't believe it is an overstatement to say that our well-being as a species lies in our ability to spot and counter misinformation.

Misinformation is both a result of and a reinforcement of all the other obstacles described in this section. Our biases, personality, cultural influences, and ignorance lead us to believe things that are not only untrue but dangerous; our embrace of misinformation keeps us from learning or letting go of our biases.

Correcting misinformation, however, means we are learning (decreasing our ignorance) and gives us a motivation and rationale for shedding our biases.

To be a clear thinker we need to be ruthless in spotting misinformation—both the mistakes or untruths that others spread and those we spread ourselves—and correcting it.

SECTION 2:

OVERCOMING THE OBSTACLES TO CLEAR THINKING

TOOLS FOR GOOD THINKING:
The ATA Clear-Thinking Framework

The good news is that there are tools we can use to overcome the five obstacles to clear thinking, and those tools are found in the ATA Clear-Thinking Framework.

Each of the obstacles has a corresponding remedy—a set of tools, attitudes, and skills. Those remedies appear on the image below and are described in the pages that follow.

TOOLS FOR CLEAR THINKING

LOGIC, SCIENTIFIC METHOD, DEBUNKING TOOLS

GENERAL KNOWLEDGE

CULTURE MAPPING

AWARENESS TO ACTION PROCESS

ANTIDOTES AND GUARDRAILS

ANTIDOTES AND GUARDRAILS

Protecting Ourselves Against Our Built-In Biases

Managing Cognitive Dissonance

Cognitive dissonance is easy to see in other people, but almost impossible to see in ourselves. We may feel the result of the dissonance—i.e., the mental stress we feel when faced with information we don't like—but our brains work to make it go away as quickly as possible, often using methods we don't recognize—the cognitive biases identified in Section 1.

Here are some simple ways to reduce the negative effects of cognitive dissonance:

- Learn to look for cognitive dissonance in yourself—the internal stress when feedback or observations rub you the wrong way for reasons you can't quite identify.
- Learn to observe cognitive dissonance in others without judgment—seeing it in action can help us see it earlier in ourselves.
- Avoid the temptation to flatly reject ideas that don't fit your worldview. Explore, with an open mind, ideas you are tempted to flatly reject.
- Avoid either/or thinking—the giver of feedback may be biased AND you may still have the flaws he identified; the product may be ahead of its time AND it may still have some flaws, etc.

Skepticism

The ability to think clearly relies partly on attitude and partly on having the requisite skills and tools.

The attitude required for clear thinking is *skepticism*.

Skepticism is the attitude and practice of matching the evidence to the claim. It assumes both an open mind and a critical mind. It is a willingness to hear the other side of an argument and to change one's mind if a compelling enough argument is made, while still being committed to rigorously challenging assumptions.

Skepticism is different from cynicism, which has come to mean the automatic dismissal of the new or strange. While cynicism starts with a closed mind, skepticism starts with an open mind and a clear-eyed willingness to question even one's own most cherished beliefs and assumptions.

The patron saint of skepticism is the Scottish enlightenment philosopher David Hume, who asserted that we really can't KNOW anything for sure but that a "wise man [or woman] proportions his belief to the evidence." The late scientist and educator Carl Sagan popularized a version of Hume's statement as "extraordinary claims require extraordinary evidence."

Skepticism begins with assessing the plausibility of a claim: Given what we already know, how likely is it that a particular claim is true? The more implausible a claim is, the more evidence we should require (and the more rigorous we should be in evaluating the validity of that evidence). Further, the consequences of a claim affect the amount of evidence we should require.

For example, if someone tells me she owns a golden retriever and shows me a picture of herself with a golden retriever, I don't need a lot of evidence to provisionally believe her. If I know she has a tendency to lie, I may hold some doubt, but it is not implausible that someone owns a golden retriever. And since the consequences related to whether or not she owns a golden retriever are minimal, I would not feel the need to seek a lot of evidence to support her claim.

It would be different, however, if someone tells me they can cure cancer by waving their healing hands over a person. Such a claim is highly implausible given what we know about science and cancer, and the consequences of someone seeking "healing hands" treatment for cancer are dire. I would require a LOT of evidence before believing such claims.

If we want to be good critical thinkers and claim to be seekers after truth, we should cultivate appropriate skepticism and remember Carl Sagan's other famous quote: "It pays to keep an open mind, but not so open that your brains fall out."

Once the right attitude is in place, some fundamental tools are helpful; the rest of this volume provides some of those tools.

The Magic Question: How do I know this to be true?

The best way to maintain appropriate skepticism is to constantly ask ourselves "How do I know this to be true?" and to be *willing to prove ourselves wrong*. Physicist Richard Feynman famously said "It is important that you don't fool yourself, and you are the easiest person to fool." We must remember this, and always challenge our assumptions and beliefs. The more strongly we believe something or the more emotion we feel about a belief, the more important it is to ask ourselves "How do I know this to be true?"

Falsification

The scientific method relies on four steps: Observation, creating a hypothesis, attempting falsify our hypothesis, and adjusting our hypothesis accordingly.

The key step is the attempt to prove ourselves wrong rather than to prove ourselves right. This attempt at falsification is one of the things that separates science from pseudoscience or mere debate.

Related to the question, "How do I know this to be true?", the effort to prove ourselves wrong should be at the heart of every critical thinker's toolkit, and they should remember that every time they have proven themselves wrong they have learned something new.

Checklists

Doctors do it, pilots do it—when lives are on the line, people use checklists. People tend to rely on their memories when they have a series of tasks to complete, but our memories are notoriously flawed and our attention is remarkably short. Important processes benefit from the creation of checklists.

Occam's Razor

Named after medieval philosopher William of Ockham, Occam's Razor is another name for the principle of parsimony—the principle that we should keep explanations as simple as possible (but no simpler!) Commonly misunderstood as meaning that the simplest answer is usually the correct answer, Occam's Razor actually encourages us to not add factors unnecessarily. If we can adequately explain a phenomenon with two factors, we shouldn't add a third.

For example, if we want to explain how ice forms, the first equation below is better than the second.

$$Ice = Water + Cold$$

$$Ice = Water + Cold + Ice\text{-}making\ fairies$$

Hanlon's Razor

"Never attribute to malice that which can be attributed to stupidity."

It is easy to assume bad intentions from others when we are overlooked or wronged. Often, however, such things are explained by mistakes rather than ill-intent. Hanlon's Razor reminds us to calm down, take a deep breath, and give people who appear to have wronged us the benefit of the doubt.

Thinking Backward

Thinking about how we don't want things to go can help us plan to avoid those outcomes. Known as "inversion," thinking backward from an envisioned outcome can help us get to the outcomes we want and avoid the outcomes we don't.

Second-Order Thinking

Unintended or unforeseen consequences are often the result of our decisions. Unfortunately, we often don't take the time to consider what such consequences might be. We make a decision to try to resolve an immediate problem, but fail to ask, "But then what?" Second-order thinking involves taking the time to think through the consequences of our actions and preparing for them.

Probabilistic Thinking

Very little in life is deterministic and we can rarely make predictions with great certainty. We do better, however, when we get into the habit of thinking in terms of probabilities—how likely is it that a thing will occur—and continue to update the odds as new data becomes available.

Avoid Unjustified Leaps of Inference

An unjustified leap of inference is drawing a conclusion that may not necessarily flow from the premises used to arrive at that conclusion. For example, just because I can safely jump off a curb or jump off a chair does not mean I can safely jump off a cliff. Assuming I could do so would be a leap too far.

When evaluating a conclusion or chain of reasoning, it is important to evaluate that each step is justified by the previous step.

Learn to Distinguish Between Naïve Intuition and Expert Intuition

System 1 thinking inclines us to trust our intuition, even if our intuition is not accurate. There is a distinct difference between naïve intuition—intuition that is based on uninformed "gut" feelings—and skilled intuition—the kind of non-conscious expertise that is the result of extensive training and experience.

If you've ever seriously studied or trained in a physical, artistic, or even intellectual pursuit, you know that after a lot of practice things that initially seemed difficult and required a lot of conscious effort became intuitive and automatic after time. This is because you trained your mind and your muscles to non-consciously act, but these actions were based on practiced expertise.

Unfortunately, the mind cannot always tell the difference between the feeling of this kind of skillful expertise and the illusory feeling of expertise in an area in which we have no trained competence. For example, because we develop the capacity to intuitively read the emotions and moods of people we know well based on repeated experience, we tend to falsely believe we can intuit the moods and needs of people we have just met. This same phenomenon is found in many areas.

Intuition is a useful and critical part of our nature, but we have to remember that there is a difference between skillful intuition based on experience and practice and potentially dangerous naïve intuition based on nothing but a false feeling of competence.

THE AWARENESS TO ACTION PROCESS

Addressing Personality Biases by Rewriting the Personality's Story

Our personality is rooted in a system of narratives centered on a specific preferred strategy. In order to help overcome the filters of our Enneagram-type strategy, we need to understand how it shapes those narratives and how we can change them in a way that allows us to incorporate new perspectives and behaviors.

We can do this through the "Awareness to Action Process."

The steps of that process are:

- Pay attention to our personality patterns and create a goal for change.
- Expose and resolve the conflicting commitments caused by the desire for change clashing with our existing narratives.
- Execute a simple but very clear action plan to embed the new attitudes in our mind.

Below is a description of how we can use this process to create change in both perspective and behavior using the Awareness to Action Process and the Enneagram. It focuses on one personality style as an example, but the same principles can be applied to all of the nine styles.

Creating Change with the Awareness to Action Process

Most advice on how to change is very straightforward (and simplistic): Become aware of your patterns and what you need to do differently, then make a plan for doing the new behavior. Of course, if it were that easy, everyone would keep their New Year's resolutions and the whole self-help industry would fade into irrelevance.

We all know that change is not easy. The reason that most attempts to change fail is because they overlook a critical step between "become aware" and "act in a new way"–they fail to resolve the internal conflicts created by the attempt to change.

As Robert Kegan and Lisa Laskow Lahey point out in their work on immunity to change, attempts to change create competing commitments in our psyche. Intellectually, we know we should change and that the change would be good for us, but we also have an old narrative that tells us that what we are currently doing is *also* good for us in some way.

The old behavior has the advantage of being comfortable and familiar, while the intended change is new and its value is not yet proven. Our internal non-conscious narrative is that the old behavior has been effective, and changing will make us less effective in some way. The change we wish to make often seems to be in conflict with our narrative, and thus seems illogical. When we attempt to change, we face a conflict: we want to change but, deep down, the change doesn't really make sense to us.

Kegan and Lahey point out that rewriting our narrative in a way that incorporates both the existing commitment *and* the new commitment is the only way to overcome the inner conflict that causes our immunity to change. The beauty of the Enneagram model of personality styles is that it tells us exactly what those narratives are based on–nine adaptive strategies and our habitual definitions of them–making it easier to rewrite them.

Before exploring this further, let's back up see how these narratives take root.

Fortunately, we humans have a great ability to function on autopilot. Life is complicated, filled with mundane tasks as well as complex activities that require our attention. In order to have time to think about the complex issues, we have evolved the ability to "outsource" the mundane to our internal autopilot.

How much could we get done if we really had to be fully conscious and present when we were tying our shoes or brushing our teeth in the morning, feeding the dog, and packing the kids' lunch, and didn't allow ourselves to think about when we have to pick up our children from school and which event to taxi them to in the evening, the project due at work, what bills need to be paid, how we will deal with the care of our aging parents, or any of the other myriad of concerns that require our attention more than our shoelaces?

Much of the day, for many of the things we do, we just need to trust our autopilot.

But while there many benefits, there are also downsides to this ability to be on autopilot–we sometimes miss our exit on the highway because our minds are elsewhere, we are lost in thought and forget our briefcase, we leave our dry-cleaning at the pre-school and our preschooler at the dry-cleaners...

When we realize that we have made one of these blunders, we are filled with a moment of anxiety or uncertainty (or downright terror, in the case of the dry-cleaning and preschool), and we immediately seek to create a narrative that resolves the situation in our mind and allows us to go back to functioning on autopilot. We "wake up" on the highway and are not sure how we got to where we are, so we look for signs or landmarks that help us locate ourselves; we remind ourselves that we are busy and we'll find a way to function without the briefcase; we blame our wife for assuming we could manage two things at once... We eventually return to our zoned-out bliss, comfortable with our story.

So, how do we change?

The inertia of habituated behavior is strong; our habitual narratives give us a sense (often false) of order and direction. Our narratives create resistance to change, and attempts to change that violate the logic of our narratives are rejected the same way the body rejects a transplanted organ of the wrong blood type.

The only way to change behavior over the long term is to change the narrative. However, we can't simply abandon a narrative that has, in many ways, worked for us for much of our lives; we have to revise it so that it honors the past and our existing values while becoming more accurate given our current circumstances. We have to create a narrative that is more authentic.

The Enneagram can help us do just that, because it tells us what is at the core of our narratives—an adaptive strategy that shapes the way we think, feel, and behave. Unfortunately, that strategy is often defined in narrow and restricting ways; what was once adaptive can now be maladaptive. Attempts to change often conflict with the existing definition of the strategy and meet resistance. If we want to change, the only way we can make the narrative more authentic is to redefine our preferred strategy in more adaptive ways.

The steps to creating change are not simple "awareness" and "action;" if we want to change we must address the crucial middle step—"authenticity."

Let's look at an example.

One of the typical issues that my Ennea-type Three clients have to work on is their ability to develop and delegate to subordinates. Their preferred adaptive strategy is "striving to feel outstanding." They have an affective need to feel like they are high-achieving and meeting the high expectations they set for themselves and have internalized from others. This affective need makes them think in ways that have to do with how outstanding they are and how they can be more outstanding. The way they think shapes the way they behave and they try to behave in ways that will make them feel more outstanding. This, of course, is not the only motivation of Threes, but it is a strong one.

A common theme for my Three clients is that they rose to their level of success by being outstanding "doers"—working harder and faster than others, demonstrating superior performance. They are the classic achievers that David McClelland wrote about in his work on motivation theory—people driven to set goals and achieve them, to be admired by others, to meet or exceed the ideals of the community.

Their habitual narrative is often rooted in an attachment to be seen as outstanding doer, and this can be their undoing as they rise to higher levels of leadership responsibility. Throughout their lives they have defined what it means to be "outstanding" as doing things better than other people. This narrow definition of the strategy has become calcified and rote. In their need to achieve they find it more satisfactory to do a task themselves rather than to take the time to teach others to do it and then delegate, even if this means that they end up with more and more work to do. The pattern becomes unsustainable as their responsibility grows and they can eventually burn out or fail to meet the commitments they have taken on.

It would be easy to say to these leaders, "Stop doing it yourself, develop your team and delegate to them." If you did give them that advice, they would nod their heads and agree that it makes sense. They might even try it for a while. But quickly the inner conflict will undermine their efforts because the new behavior seems to undermine their narrowly defined implicit strategy. They ask, How can I perform better than others or strive for high standards of accomplishment if I take time out to teach other people how to do something? I will probably just have to redo it anyway because the other person surely won't do it as well as I could have done it. Therefore, it just makes sense to do it myself.

Someone who does not have this same preferred strategy is working on a different model of logic and may easily see the flaws in this line of thinking. But each of us can get trapped by our narrative and be blind to what seems obvious to others.

In order to change, the Three leader must revise their narrative and rewrite the preferred strategy. In this case, they would recognize that their restrictive, calcified narrative is outdated and maladaptive and they would revise the strategy at its core to something along the lines of "Instead of being an outstanding doer, I will strive to be an outstanding leader. Outstanding leaders do the following things: develop people, delegate effectively so they can work at higher levels...."

If the Three can see that the change they want to make can help them actually satisfy a fundamental value (being outstanding), not undermine it, their non-conscious narratives will not create obstacles to the change. When the strategy is redefined and the narrative rewritten in such a way, I find that the client actually wants to make the change and undertakes the action plan eagerly. The conflict between the inner commitments is resolved.

Taken together, the Awareness to Action Process looks like this:

1. *Awareness*: Pay attention. Recognize your habitual patterns. Set a goal for change.
2. *Authenticity*: Identify the conflicting commitments created by the change. Rewrite your narrative by redefining the preferred strategy in a way that honors your existing values *and* makes the change attractive.
3. *Action*: Create a simple and specific action plan. Deliberately practice the new behaviors to resist reverting back to old narratives.
4. Repeat!

While the missing piece of most change efforts is found in the "authenticity" step, we must also realize that this is an ongoing activity. We can't just rewrite the narrative once, since all narratives are limited and, by their nature, eventually become outdated.

We should be constantly redefining the strategy—challenging our assumptions and dismantling our defenses and resistance, venturing farther from our traditional comfort zones. The word "authenticity" has the same root as the word "author." Being authentic in this case means taking control of our narratives and being the author of our own lives; writing a story that is more aligned with our current reality than our habituated past.

Rather than allowing our narratives and our implicit definition of our strategy to be calcified and bounded, we should constantly work on clarifying the definition of the strategy, making it permeable so that it gradually includes more and more possibilities. Sticking with the example of the Three Leader, constantly challenging and reshaping the implicit definition of striving to feel outstanding eventually leads to a definition of outstanding that includes one who has given up on such strivings. This is the path to freedom from the grip of the calcified strategy.

Yes, our implicit limited and calcified definitions of the strategy are often used in ineffective or outdated ways; the strategy is a lens that can easily become covered with mud and grime. But we do not need to abandon it completely. It is our nature to habitually view life through some lens or adopt some strategy. It makes no sense to reinvent the wheel for each new circumstance; life is easier when we find a strategy that works for us and work on clarifying it.

But we must continually polish and clean the lens; the strategy must serve us rather than us becoming a slave to it. While the implicit strategy is bound and calcified, treating it like clay or dough to be kneaded and stretched allows it to become permeable and frees us to use other strategies without feeling like we have lost something we can't live without.

Over time, the strategy transforms from resembling a steel ring that restrains us to seeming like the expansive and fluid ripples on the surface of a pond. The outstanding doer becomes the outstanding leader as she understands that it is empowering others that leads to true greatness. She understands that the outstanding careerist can become the outstanding parent or spouse. It begins to take hold that the truly outstanding person is motivated by higher values than the perceptions and judgments of other people, and that the most outstanding person you can be is to simply be your authentic self.

Effective, lasting change begins with working with the preferred strategy–simultaneously challenging it, embracing it and reclaiming it from the shadow, redefining it in adaptive ways that serve us rather than restrict us. Ignoring the "authenticity" step in the Awareness to Action process is to miss the whole point and to set ourselves up for failure on the path to change.

IDENTIFYING CULTURAL BIAS

Culture and the biases that arise from it are a broad topic and we cannot really do justice to it in this slim volume so I am including only a few thoughts. Culture is shaped by many forces, but there are some good questions with which to start.

We can begin to examine group or individual cultural biases based on the factors below. Doing so allows us to bring implicit assumptions to the surface and explore the impact they have on the group, or how they may impede your thinking.

- *Time orientation*—are we in clock or event time?
- *Power distance*—do we obey or challenge our leaders?
- *Uncertainty avoidance*—do we avoid uncertainty or embrace it?
- *Individualism*—are we collectivist or individualist?
- *High/low context*—do we communicate explicitly or implicitly
- *Instinctual biases*—which instinctual bias shapes us?
- *Modal personality style*—which Enneagram strategy holds sway?

Some excellent books on culture are listed in the resources at the back of this book and I encourage you to explore them further.

GENERAL KNOWLEDGE

Overcoming Ignorance

We live in a time when practically all the information in the world is available, literally, in the palm of our hand thanks to technology. Some see this as a reason not to pursue a general education—why bother learning thinks outside my immediate concerns if I can find out anything I need at any time I need to find it?

The value of a general education is that it gives us context, and context allows us to see connections between facts that others miss. Without context, we often don't know what we don't know, and we don't know that we should look for information that we don't have. Context allows us to know when something is important and deserves more attention or deeper inquiry. Broad general knowledge serves as an early warning system to both danger and opportunity.

Finally, general knowledge adds richness to life. People who do not recognize a reference to Shakespeare or understand the context of the Gettysburg Address will have a superficial appreciation of those things. Like a color-blind person, they may be able to function fine, but their experience will be greatly diminished.

Craft a Relevant Learning Plans to Foster a Foundation of General Knowledge

Once out of college, we are responsible for crafting and following our own learning plans. A good general-knowledge education should address the following:

- Basic Science
- Basic Philosophy
- Basic World Literature
- Basic Religious Literacy
- Basic Mathematics
- Basic Arts Literacy
- Etc.

Putting Together Your Curriculum

Everyone's interests and needs are different and a good liberal arts education is broad while allowing one to go deeper in areas of particular interest. In the rest of this chapter I will recommend some classics as well as some general overviews of a particular topic. The reader is encouraged to dive in deeper when curiosity strikes.

Biography and History

Many leaders want to learn by example from great leaders, so they turn to biography when they become bored with leadership self-help books. Biographies of great leaders can be very informative, and authors such as Robert Caro, Jon Meacham, Ron Chernow, Edmund Morris, Doris Kearns Goodwin, and David McCullough can weave riveting tales. The thing to remember about biographies of great leaders, however, is that what worked for them may not necessarily work for you. Sometimes leaders succeed despite themselves, and sometimes their success was situational. A case in point is Churchill, whose leadership style was masterful during wartime but less so during peace. That said, reading biographies can be very informative, and one quickly finds that there are very few novel situations; if you are facing a leadership challenge, there is a good chance that someone has faced it before and learning how they met the challenge can save you a lot of headache and heartache.

Even more useful than reading biographies of great leaders, perhaps, is reading history. History provides context, and any piece of data is more useful when we understand the context. Companies often worry about losing tribal knowledge and try to manage their workforce so that all the senior workers, who carry that knowledge, don't leave at the same time. Someone has to educate the newer people. Part of being a leader is understanding the external forces that shape, hinder, or help the business.

Not understanding history is the same as losing tribal knowledge in a workforce–understanding the context enables one to address circumstances more effectively. My favorite brief history overview is E.H. Gombrich's "A Little History of the World." I frequently encourage clients to pick an era and region that is of particular interest to them and dig in, and to find an author who holds their attention and read a few of his or her books. It is hard to go wrong with Barbara Tuchman, Theodore White, William Dalrymple, Peter Ackroyd, and Simon Schama.

The Hard Sciences

Most leaders seem more comfortable with the hard sciences than with the soft sciences. That said, rounding out one's scientific literacy is as useful as it is intellectually stimulating. Natalie Angier's "The Canon: A Whirligig Tour of the Beautiful Basics of Science" and Hazen and Trefil's "Science Matters: Achieving Scientific Literacy" are my favorite primers. I recently began reading William Bynum's "A Little History of Science" and am enjoying it as well. I tend to be drawn to the biological sciences, and always recommend that any thinking person develop a better understanding of Darwin's theory of natural selection, widely considered by scientists to be the most important idea, ever. One of my favorite introductions is David Sloan Wilson's "Evolution for Everyone: How Darwin's Theory Can Change the Way We Think About Our Lives."

When it comes to physics, it is hard to beat Richard Feynman. Try "The Character of Physical Law" as a starting point. I also enjoyed Feynman's essays on the nature of science, "The Meaning of It All." And, while I've never been able to wrap my head around relativity, I've found Albert Einstein's "Ideas and Opinions" to be riveting. Einstein demonstrates that, despite the stereotype, brilliant people need not be socially inept or narrow in scope.

Philosophy

Though Feynman, in particular, would never admit it, these last two works are better thought of as philosophy than hard science, and I think philosophy is the discipline most neglected by leaders. It is philosophy that teaches us how to think about the facts we learn, how to test ideas, how to order knowledge. It is philosophy that teaches us how to think critically, and every great leader I have known is a rigorous critical-thinker. Nigel Wharburton's "A Little History of Philosophy" (see what Gombrich started...) is a great introduction, as is his podcast "Philosophy Bites." Since our view of the world influences how we lead others in it, being conscious of one's philosophical assumptions is a critical rite of passage for leaders. Every leader should wrestle with the implications of Plato's "Republic," for example, or Machiavelli's "The Prince." (I recommend reading about "The Republic" before trying to tackle the original; and Simon Blackburn is a good start.) I also think a book like Jim Holt's "Why Does the World Exist: An Existential Detective Story" forces us to think about questions and challenge our assumptions.

Finally, the philosopher who I think every thoughtful person should be acquainted with is David Hume. Few minds had the clarity of Hume or the impact on the modern sensibility that he did. Again, Blackburn provides a good introduction.

Psychology

"Amateur psychologist" is one of the hats that every leader must wear. While familiarity with theorists such as Freud, Jung, Adler, et al is useful, I think that more recent developments in the cognitive sciences are more valuable for leaders. I recommend "The Wisest One in the Room" by Thomas Gilovich and Lee Ross and Tavris and Aronson's "Mistakes Were Made (but not by me)."

Mythology, Religion, and the Classics

Once, over dinner in a small town outside of Frankfurt, a client recommended that on my next visit I stay at a place called Hotel Bacchus. I replied that I would; "After all, any hotel named after the god of wine and fertility must be a great place," I joked. My host was taken aback and laughed. "Sorry," he said, "I'm just shocked to meet an American who knows who Bacchus was."

To be a truly educated person, one should have at least a passing familiarity with mythology, religion, and the classics. Most of our culture is based on mythological stories of the gods, sacred texts, and the writings of Shakespeare, Homer, Ovid, etc. Ignorance of these underpinnings of culture is akin to being color blind; we see, but we lose the subtleties and the richness. Start with Joseph Campbell's "Myths to Live By" and "The Power of Myth" (which is also available as a video. I also recommend Stephen Prothero's "Religious Literacy." (I'll note, by the way, that while Hotel Bacchus was a very pleasant hotel, there was nothing particularly bacchanalian about it.)

Being Global

Today's global economy requires that all senior leaders must be global in their outlook. There are many useful books available on understanding different cultures, but among my favorites are Trompenaars and Hampden-Turner's "Riding the Waves of Culture," Hooker's "Working Across Cultures," and Cabrera and Unruh's "Being Global." I also recommend international news publications such as the *Financial Times*, *The Economist*, and *Foreign Policy*, all of which have excellent apps and online editions.

Being global also means that many senior leaders travel extensively. Most of these trips are short and there is little spare time. However, I think it is critically important to occasionally allow for time to visit the places we are flying in and out of.

A liberal arts education is incomplete without the inclusion of culture and travel allows for exposure to experiences one cannot get in any other way.

Learn a few words of the local language, eat the local foods, visit museums and places of worship. It is one thing to see the Mona Lisa in a book; it is wholly another to stand in front of her. One cannot be unchanged standing in Paris's Pantheon, wandering through Istanbul's Blue Mosque or Cairo's Sultan Hassan Mosque, basking in the radiant colors of the El Grecos in Madrid's Prado, or walking into Florence's Santa Croce Cathedral and seeing the sarcophaguses of Michelangelo, Machiavelli, Rossini, and Galileo.

Beyond Books

Of course, there are other ways to learn. Most senior leaders don't have the time to take classes, but downloadable lectures and audiobooks are easily available. I like *The Great Courses* and Audible.com, and the free podcasts available on iTunes are a treasure trove.

The joy of a broad general education is that it presents life as an endless buffet. This list of recommendations is short and as notable for what it doesn't include as for what it does (I can't help but notice that it is English language- and US-centric; *c'est la vie*). Half the fun is designing your own curriculum and I hope this helps you get started.

GUARDING AGAINST MISINFORMATION

Logic, the Scientific Method, and the Boloney-Detection Kit

Your Network of Tools and Models

A good "boloney-detection kit" helps us navigate life without being deceived—either by others or ourselves. It involves creating a network of critical-thinking tools and mental models that help us filter the ocean of information that comes our way each day.

Creating a good boloney-detection kit involves picking a tool, model, or concept in each of the five thinking domains and practicing them. Start with one practice in each domain and add from there.

In addition to development of skill in the tools, you should ask yourself two questions whenever you encounter information or assertions:

- Is this a *belief/feeling* question or a *fact* question? (Remember, this is the heart of epistemic clarity.)
- If the latter, am I exercising appropriate skepticism?

Spotting Pseudoscience and Pseudo-expertise

The world is awash in pseudo-science and pseudo-experts ("pseudo" means "false") and it can be difficult to tell the difference. Here are some things to watch for when trying to spot nonsense and those who would peddle it.

- The use of vague, exaggerated, or untestable claims.
- Reliance on confirming evidence rather than falsification.
- Resistance to having their claims tested by other experts.

- A lack of progress in the field, and the dependence on dogma and tradition rather than exploration and expansion.
- Personalizing issues and demonizing critics or competitors. (Claims of persecution or conspiracy from "outsiders" or "Big _____" mainstreamers.)
- Use of misleading, vague, or ambiguous language. (Creating unnecessary neo-logisms, "science-y" sounding terms, or idiosyncratic definitions of existing terms.)
- Blurring the boundaries of one's expertise (physicists making assertions about climate; chiropractors making claims about vaccines; medical doctors making claims about physics; etc.
- Reliance on testimonials and anecdotes rather than evidence.
- The Galileo Gambit—claiming to be a misunderstood genius whenever their claims or credibility are challenged.
- Use of the "Gish Gallop"—avoiding critique by spewing out fallacies faster than they can be debunked to overwhelm challengers.
- Over-confidence and lack of humility. Real scientists know that all science is provisional— only good until new evidence comes along.
- Use of the term "scientifically proven." (Science doesn't actually "prove" anything to be true, it either proves something untrue or determines probabilities of accuracy.)
- Reliance on and repetition of discredited or disproved ideas.
- Invocation of vague, untested, or untestable "energies."
- Pointing to post-hoc, phony patterns.

Adapted from:
https://en.wikipedia.org/wiki/Pseudoscience#Classifying_pseudoscience and https://scienceornot.net/science-red-flags/

Recognizing Expertise

A real expert:

- has superior factual knowledge in the field and exceptional understanding of how to apply the facts to produce concrete results.
- has a better ability than her peers to differentiate between similar, but not identical cases.
- shows consistency in judgments that is better than her peers.
- is identified by her peers in the field as an expert.

A real expert's:

- arguments are logical and consistent.
- arguments are recognized as valid by most other experts in the field.
- expertise is vouched for by third parties that have authority in the field.
- has no conflict of interest or prejudices that may influence his or her judgments.
- has a successful track record of judgments in his or her field.

Adapted from
https://scienceornot.net/2014/06/29/trusting-the-experts/

UNDERSTANDING LOGICAL FALLACIES

Learning to recognize logical fallacies in the arguments of others makes us more disciplined in being logical ourselves.

Informal logical fallacies, like those on the following pages, do not necessarily invalidate an argument, but they are fallacious because they cannot serve *alone* as sufficient justification for a point of view.

Common Logical Fallacies

- *Ad hominem*: attacking the person rather than the merit of the idea they are proposing.
- *Appeal to antiquity or custom*: giving undue validity to an argument because it is old or part of a tradition.
- *Appeal to authority*: giving undue validity to an argument because an important or famous person made it.
- *Appeal to emotion*: encouraging people to focus on their feelings rather than the facts when evaluating an argument.
- *Appeal to popularity*: claiming that an argument is valid because a lot of people believe it.
- *Appeal to the stone*: dismissing a claim as absurd without providing proof for its absurdity.
- *Argument from ignorance*: assuming that a claim is true because it has not been or cannot be proven false, or vice versa.
- *Argument from incredulity*: "I cannot imagine how this could be true; therefore, it must be false."
- *Begging the question*: providing the conclusion of the argument as a premise.
- *Shifting the burden of proof*: claiming, I need not prove my claim, you must prove it is false.
- *Circular reasoning*: when the reasoner begins with what he or she is trying to end up with; sometimes called assuming the conclusion.

- *Circular cause and consequence*: when the consequence of the phenomenon is claimed to be its root cause.
- *Correlation proves causation* (also known as *post hoc ergo propter hoc,* "after the thing, therefore because of the thing"): a flawed assumption that because there is a correlation between two variables that one caused the other.
- *False authority*: elevating an expert of dubious credentials or using only one opinion to promote a product or idea.
- *False choice*: when two contrasting statements are held to be the only possible options when in reality there are more.
- *False equivalence*: assuming logical and apparent equivalence when in fact there is none.
- *Fallacy of the single cause*: assuming there is one simple cause of an outcome when in it may have actually been caused by a number of interrelated causes.
- *Inflation of conflict*: assuming that if experts disagree on a certain point, the scholars of a whole field must not know anything.
- *McNamara fallacy (quantitative fallacy)*: making a decision based only on quantitative observations and discounting all other considerations.
- *Moving the goalposts*: an argument in which the evidence presented in response to a specific claim is dismissed with a demand for some other (often greater) evidence.
- *Naturalistic fallacy*: inferring the something is good because it is the way it is now or it is the way it was in the past.
- *Shifting the burden of proof*: assuming that the person questioning a claim is responsible for proving the validity of the claim, rather than assuming the burden is on the person making the claim.
- *Proof by assertion*: repeatedly restating a proposition regardless of contradiction.

- *Proof by verbosity*: overwhelming others with an argument too complex and verbose to reasonably deal with in all its details.
- *Prosecutor's fallacy*: a low probability of false matches does not mean a low probability of some false match being found.
- *Psychologist's fallacy*: presupposes the objectivity of one's own perspective when analyzing a behavioral event.
- *Red herring*: an attempt to distract an audience by deviating from the topic at hand with a separate argument the speaker believes is easier to address.
- *Reification*: when an abstraction is treated as if it were a concrete, real event or physical entity.
- *Shotgun argumentation*: the arguer offers such a large number of arguments for a position that the opponent can't possibly respond to all of them.
- *Special pleading*: when an advocate of a position attempts to cite an exemption to a generally accepted rule or principle without justifying the exemption.
- *Straw Man*: Misrepresenting another's claim and then attacking the misrepresentation rather than the actual point being made.
- *Tu quoque*: "You did it too." Pointing out another person's error or transgression rather than addressing your own. Also known as "What about-ism."

DECISION-MAKING TOOLS: *SOME ADDITIONS TO YOUR TOOLKIT*

The ATA Questionnaire

The ATA Questionnaire is a simple, broad set of questions to prime our thinking when evaluating an important decision. It is meant to help narrow down the focus of what other decision-making tools need to be implemented before taking a plan of action.

- What biases am I falling victim to?
- How is my personality shaping my assumptions?
- What cultural factors are at play?
- What information am I missing?
- What logical errors am I making?

Decision-Making Conceptual Tools

- *Regression to the Mean*—Over time, averages return to the mean; deviations tend to be anomalies and we should not over react to them.
- *Pareto Principle*—In general, 80% of our results come from 20% of our efforts, so it is good to find and emphasize that 20%.
- *Gresham's Law*—Forged currency drives out legitimate currency; in most fields, low-quality product eventually drives out high-quality product.
- *Tragedy of the Commons*—If someone takes more than their share of communal resources, everyone else will do the same.
- *The Network Effect*—A system becomes more valuable as more nodes or elements are added to it. You are more effective if you are connected to more people who could provide value.
- *Via negativa vs. via positive*—Solving problems by subtraction of factors vs solving problems by addition of factors.

- *Randomness*—Life is more random than it appears and we must not infer patterns or signals where they don't exist.
- *Compounding*—Efforts should add compounding (i.e., ongoing and increasing) value.
- *Multiplying by Zero*—If one piece of the chain is a zero, the sum will be zero. One incompetent person brings down the whole team.
- *Laws of Small and Large Numbers*—Large samples are more reliable than small samples.
- *The Bell Curve*—Most data sets contain lower numbers at the extremes and higher numbers nearer the mean.
- *Bayesian Updating*—We should change our assessment of the odds of something occurring as new information becomes available.

The After-Action Analysis

An After-Action Analysis is exactly what it sounds like: an analysis of an activity in an attempt to improve future performance of the same activity.

The process is very simple:

- Without judgement, evaluate a recent activity by answering the following questions:
- What went well? Did we do anything that can serve as a repeatable best practice?
- What did not go well? How can we ensure that we don't repeat it?
- What can we do better next time?

The Pre-Mortem Exercise

The opposite of the after-action analysis, this is a tool to help identify potential pitfalls and obstacles in advance of an initiative.

- Think of one important goal you have for the next year.
- Look at it and visualize yourself having failed to achieve it at the end of the year.
- List all the possible reasons for that failure.
- Break your list into four categories: 1. Things I did, 2. Things I didn't do, 3. Things others did, and 4. Things others didn't do.
- Plan to mitigate possible sources of failure.

The OODA Loop

Developed by Air Force Colonel and military strategist John Boyd, the OODA loop is a way of testing action to ensure constant improvement. "OODA" stands for observe, orient, decide, and act. While it requires a great deal of rigor to apply, the steps are simple:

- *Observe*: Gather and organize all relevant information.
- *Orient*: Filter the information through relevant mental models, such as the many models in this guidebook.
- *Decide*: Create an actionable hypothesis.
- *Act*: Test the hypothesis through trial.
- Repeat as necessary by observing results of the trial.

RESOURCES

Cognitive Science:

- Aronson, Elliot and Carol Tavris, "Mistakes Were Made (But Not by Me): Why We Justify Foolish Beliefs, Bad Decisions, and Hurtful Acts"
- Gilovich, Thomas and Lee Ross, "The Wisest One in the Room: How You Can Benefit From Social Psychology's Most Powerful Insights"
- Haidt, Jonathan, "The Happiness Hypothesis"
- Kahneman, Daniel, "Thinking Fast and Slow"
- Thaler, Richard, "Misbehaving: The Making of Behavioral Economics"
- Sunstein, Cass, "Wiser: Getting Beyond Group Think to Make Groups Smarter"
- Wilson, Timothy, "Strangers to Ourselves"
- Hood, Bruce, "The Science of Superstition"
- Lilienfeld, Lynn, Ruscio, and Beyerstein, "50 Great Myths of Popular Psychology"
- Burton, Robert, "On Being Certain: Believing You Are Right Even When You're Not"
- Stanovich, Keith "The Robot's Rebellion"
- Wood, Jennifer, "20 Cognitive Biases That Affect Your Decisions," http://mentalfloss.com/us/go/68705
- Wilke, A and R Mata, "Cognitive Bias," The Encyclopedia of Human Behavior, http://people.clarkson.edu/~awilke/Research_files/EoHB_Wilke_12.pdf
- Sperber, Dan, and Hugo Mercier, "The Enigma of Reason"
- "The Argumentative Theory—A Conversation with Hugo Mercier," http://edge.org/conversation/hugo_mercier-the-argumentative-theory
- Sperber, Dan and Hugo Mercier, "Why Do Humans Reason? Arguments for an Argumentative Theory," https://hal.archives-ouvertes.fr/hal-00904097/document.
- Trivers, Robert, "The Folly of Fools"

- Galinsky, Adam and Maurice Schweitzer, "Friend & Foe: When to Cooperate, When to Compete, and How to Succeed at Both."

Personality Styles

- www.AbouttheEnneagram.com
- Tallon, Robert and Mario Sikora, "Awareness to Action: The Enneagram, Emotional Intelligence, and Change"
- Barondes, Samuel, "Making Sense of People: Decoding the Mysteries of Personality"

Culture

- Trompenaars, Fons, and Charles Hampden-Turner, "Riding the Waves of Culture: Understanding Diversity in Global Business"
- Cabrera, Angel, and Gregory Unruh, "Being Global: How to Think, Act, and Lead in a Transformed World"
- Hofstede, Geert, and Gert Jan Hofstede, "Cultures and Organizations: Software of the Mind"
- Lewis, Richard D., "When Cultures Collide: Leading Across Cultures"
- Hooker, John, "Working Across Cultures"
- Cabrera, Angel, and Gregory Unruh, "Being Global"
- Steves, Rick, "Travel as a Political Act"

Knowledge

- Grazer, Brian and Charles Fishman, "A Curious Mind"
- Bazerman, Max, "The Power of Noticing"
- Poundstone, William, "Head in the Cloud"
- Suzuki, Shunryu, "Zen Mind, Beginner's Mind"

- Angier, Natalie, "The Canon: A Whirligig Tour of the Beautiful Basics of Science"
- Shermer, Michael, "Why Darwin Matters"
- Gombrich, E.H., "A Little History of the World
- Hazen and Trefil, Science Matters: Achieving Scientific Literacy"
- Bynum, William, "A Little History of Science"
- Wilson, David Sloan, "Evolution for Everyone: How Darwin's Theory Can Change the Way We Think About Our Lives"
- Feynman, Richard, "The Character of Physical Law"
- Feynman, Richard, "The Meaning of It All"
- Einstein, Albert, "Ideas and Opinions"
- Wharburton, Nigel, "A Little History of Philosophy"
- Plato, "The Republic"
- Blackburn, Simon, "Plato's Republic: Biography of a Book"
- Blackburn, Simon, "How to Read Hume"
- Holt, Jim, "Why Does the World Exist: An Existential Detective Story"
- Campbell, Joseph, "Myths to Live By"
- Prothero, Stephen, "Religious Literacy"

Misinformation

- The Economist Books, "Truth Counts: A Practical Guide for News Consumers"
- Ellenberg, Jordan, "How Not to Be Wrong: The Power of Mathematical Thinking"
- Pigliucci, Massimo, "Nonsense on Stilts: How to Tell Science from Bunk"
- Sagan, Carl, "Demon-Haunted World"
- Mitroff, Ian I., and Warren Bennis, "The Unreality Industry: The Deliberate Manufacturing of Falsehood and What it is Doing to our Lives"
- Thompson, Damian, "Counterknowledge: How we surrendered to conspiracy theories, quack medicine, bogus science, and fake history"
- Huff, Darrell, "How to Lie With Statistics"

- Gardner, Martin, "Science: Good, Bad, and Bogus"
- "Your Logical Fallacy Is" website, yourlogicalfallacyis.com.
- "Master List of Logical Fallacies" http://utminers.utep.edu/omwilliamson/ENGL13 11/fallacies.htm.
- Bazerman, Max H., and Dom A. Moore, "Judgement in Managerial Decision Making"
- Gilovich, Thomas, "How We Know What Isn't So"
- Simon, Herbert A., "Administrative Behavior: A Study of Decision-Making Processes in Administrative Organizations (4th Edition)"
- March, James G., "A Primer on Decision Making: How Decisions Happen"
- Paul, Richard W., and Linda Elder, "Critical Thinking: Tools for Taking Charge of Your Professional and Personal Life"
- Dennett, Daniel C., "Intuition Pumps and Other Tools for Thinking"
- Benson and Stangroom, "Why Truth Matters"

ABOUT THE AUTHOR

Mario Sikora is president of the Awareness to Action International and an executive coach and leadership-development consultant who works with leaders in organizations across the globe. A leading authority on the Enneagram model of personality style, Mario also conducts certification programs to teach the concepts contained in this book to coaches, consultants, trainers, and HR/OD professionals.

Mario's clients have included Siemens, Celgene, Dow Chemicals, Pfizer, Panasonic, Arris Inc., Rovi Corp., Motorola, TE Connectivity, and Johnson & Johnson.

He lives outside of Philadelphia with his wife and four sons.

He can be reached at mario@awarenesstoaction.com or +1.267.304.1234.

OUR PROGRAMS

*For more information, contact Mario Sikora at
mario@awarenesstoaction.com or +1.267.304.1234*

The Personalities@Work Program

Our signature program can be conducted in half-day,
full-day, and two-day versions and can be customized
for senior leaders, mid-level leaders, and front-line
leaders.

Instinctual Leadership: Half-day and Full-day Programs

Each of us has a particular instinctual focus of attention
that shapes what we value. This focus influences our
leadership style, creating strengths and blind spots.

Preserving leaders are focused on the nuts and bolts of
leadership—processes, structures, administration, etc.,
but they can be overly conservative and uninspiring.

Navigating leaders are focused on group dynamics and
culture, and they are often good strategic thinkers; but
they can struggle with execution and administration.

Transmitting leaders are focused on the intensity and
excitement of the business—selling their vision, ideas,
and products to whomever will listen—but they can
struggle to read subtle cues from others or changing
group dynamics.

The Instinctual Leadership Program explores these three
leadership styles and equips each style to leverage their
strengths and overcome the liabilities caused by their
unconscious focus of attention.

Personalities@Work: Two-day Program

Participants go even deeper in building their awareness
of personality styles and their effect on individual and
group performance in this two-day program.

The Personalities@Work program helps organizations develop their employees' skills in self-awareness and emotional intelligence, which are crucial for a successful and engaged workplace.

Personalities@Work empowers groups to improve communication and cooperation, reduce conflict, and increase appreciation for diversity by exploring the three instinctual biases and nine personality styles found in the workplace. Participants learn about their personality style, the personality styles of their coworkers, and how those styles affect every aspect of the business.

Clear-Thinking Skills and Decision-making for Leaders

Current scientific theory about how we reason suggests that we are excellent at reasoning our way to what we want to believe, but not so good at seeing the world clearly and objectively. However, we tend to believe the opposite--that our intuitions are objective and accurate. This program helps leaders develop the tools and skills they need to reduce the innate reasoning biases that tend to cloud our judgment.

While soft skills—such as emotional intelligence or the ability to manage conflict and communicate well—are critical for strong leadership, effective reasoning and decision-making skills are an important and often-overlooked part of the leader's toolkit. This program will give you those skills.

Awareness to Action Leadership: Executive Coaching Program

The Awareness to Action Leadership-Development Program helps high-potential leaders develop unparalleled self-awareness linked to execution.

The program combines an in-depth personality-style assessment, a 360-degree review, and a systematic approach in which an executive coach helps leaders:

- Identify their strengths and opportunities for growth,
- Create an action plan that helps them immediately improve performance and grow in ways that aide in career advancement, and,
- Utilize a set of leadership and performance models that set the stage for life-long learning.

Ongoing coaching sessions help ensure that leaders understand the feedback in the context of their personality style. Further, the sessions assist in developing ways of thinking that will help the client approach leadership challenges with more flexibility and effectiveness.

Awareness to Action Teams: Overcoming Resistance to Change

Awareness to Action Teams is designed for intact teams seeking to find ways to function more coherently and effectively. It begins with a thorough analysis of the developmental needs of the team and an in-depth profile of the team members using the Enneagram model of personality styles. It examines the psychological causes of resistance to change and how they can be overcome.

Once the team personality profile has been identified, we take the participants through the three-step Awareness to Action process to help the team develop the skills needed to identify a shared purpose and remove interpersonal barriers that make it difficult to achieve that purpose.

As each team is different, our consultants customize this program to meet individual customer needs and it can be used as a foundation for ongoing work.

Contact Mario Sikora at:

Email:
mario@mariosikora.com

Facebook:
www.facebook.com/mariosikorapage/

LinkedIn:
MarioLinkedIn.com

Twitter:
@mariosikora

73046070R00051

Made in the
USA
Middletown, DE